To Art & Vanessa

What a joy to see you
both in Durban for Christmas.

Much love
Chrissie X
S.A. 1996.

SOUTH AFRICA
A PICTURE MEMORY

Text
Bill Harris

Captions
Pauline Graham

Design
Teddy Hartshorn

Photography
D and AC Adams
Colour Library Books Ltd
Photo Access

Commissioning Editor
Andrew Preston

Editorial
Gill Waugh

Production
Ruth Arthur
Sally Connolly
David Proffit
Andrew Whitelaw

Director of Production
Gerald Hughes

CLB 2744
This edition published 1996 by Central News Agency Ltd,
Laub Street, New Centre, Johannesburg, South Africa.
Originally published by Colour Library Books Ltd, Godalming, Surrey, England.
© Struik Publishers (Pty) Ltd, Cape Town, South Africa.
Printed and bound by Kyodo Printing Co (Pte) Ltd, Singapore.
All rights reserved.
ISBN 0 86283 857 6

SOUTH AFRICA
A PICTURE MEMORY

It is a rare young person who doesn't believe that a diamond is the symbol of enduring love, and South Africa is one of the world's principal producers of gem diamonds. Not only that, no matter where in the world a diamond was mined or cut, its price was probably established by South African merchants who may have shared in the profit from its sale, even though both Zaire and the Soviet Union produce more diamonds than South Africa.

It all began one day in 1866 when Erasmus Jacobz was playing on his father's farm along the banks of the Orange River. He found a shiny stone there and took it home as a gift for his mother, but neither of them knew what it was until several months later when a neighbor, who knew a little something about stones, identified it as a diamond. A geologist confirmed it and told them it weighed 21.25 carats. It was a far cry from the 3,106-carat Cullinan Diamond that was discovered in the Transvaal in 1905, but it was enough to make the Jacobz family wealthy beyond their wildest dreams. Its name, "Eureka," was an inspiration to others to seek their fortunes in South Africa too. The population of the Jacobz's neighborhood increased by 50,000 virtually overnight.

The diamond rush might be compared to the gold rush that hit California a few years earlier, but in the goldfields a big nugget didn't bring instant prosperity. A prospector had to find a rich vein of gold and then work long, backbreaking hours to dig it up. However, a single diamond, small enough to carry in his pocket, might set a man up for life and the best part was that in South Africa in the 1870s they were lying on the ground. A prospector didn't even have to invest in a pick and shovel. It wasn't uncommon for some of them to show up in the new diamond fields in suits and ties – but it was rough country and, on the whole, the fortune hunters were generally a rough and tumble lot, although there was at least one notable exception.

He was an eighteen year old who had gone to South Africa from England to live on his brother's farm where it was hoped the climate would improve his frail health. His brother was more interested in diamond hunting and convinced him that if they went to New Rush, the town that eventually became Kimberly, he might be able to pick up the money he needed to go home and enroll at Oxford. He was right: Cecil Rhodes found the means of financing his own education and then he found a new purpose in life at the university. Following the lead of one of his professors, John Ruskin, Rhodes developed a passion for the idea of bringing the whole world under British rule – an idea which included the recovery of England's lost colonies in the United States and the unification of Africa under Anglo-Saxon control.

Of course, he knew that passion wasn't enough. Such a dream would take money, but he knew where to find it. His only problem was that his health was growing steadily worse and he felt that he needed to act quickly. At the same time, the diamond prospectors were facing a problem of their own.

The alluvial diamonds that had been scattered on the ground had nearly all been picked up and the only way to get more was to dig for them. More than hard work, the job called for special equipment because the gems were buried deep. Rhodes managed to raise the necessary capital, but by the time he got back to South Africa, another English entrepreneur, Barney Barnato, had also raised enough to fund the Kimberly Central Mining Company and had created a near monopoly for himself.

But Rhodes was a man with a mission. A Boer family named De Beers had become annoyed with diamond hunters trampling their crops, and when Rhodes offered to take the farm off their hands they sold it to him. It gave him a base and then he declared war on Barnato. With the help of Lord Rothschild and other European financiers, he was able to get control of the Kimberly company and merged it into his own De Beers Company. It wasn't the end of the road for Barnato, however. Along with Alfred Beit, a German diamond expert, and Rhodes himself, he became a lifetime director of the new company, which unabashedly promised it would become the most powerful company the world had ever seen.

That was Rhodes' department. Before long he became Prime Minister of the British South African Colony (much to the chagrin of the Dutch Afrikaner population that had been elbowed out by the British in 1806 and had formed their own republics of the Orange Free State and the Transvaal). Rhodes' position made it possible for him to annex the Kimberly area from under the Afrikaners' noses, and when gold deposits were discovered in Witwatersrand, he began moving toward annexing that part of the Transvaal too. It ultimately led to the Boer War, one of the bloodiest the English have ever seen, which in turn led to the creation of the Union of South Africa.

Rhodes died in 1902 as the war was drawing to a close. The unification of South African provinces as a part of the British Empire is generally considered one of his major legacies, but his gift to the Dutch-descended Afrikaners was the idea that the races could be kept apart, as the Afrikaners had been from the British.

Moreover, during Rhodes' lifetime, as the mining process became more sophisticated, skilled workers – all of them white – were brought from England to operate the expensive machinery. Manual labor was left to the blacks, supervised by white South Africans. In the early years a thriving market in contraband diamonds smuggled out from the mines caused prices to be depressed. The company attacked the problem by requiring black workers to remain within the mining compounds for the duration of their contracts and by carefully searching all of them at the end of each shift. Blacks were also forbidden to engage in mining on their own, and possession of a diamond usually led to imprisonment and sometimes even to death. Slavery had been abolished in South Africa a half-century earlier, but the law didn't seem to apply to these miners who had signed contracts and were well paid. A contract and salary meant that their status couldn't be considered slavery. But, notwithstanding, they were still separated from their families, were virtual prisoners in their jobs and the white workers were not subject to the same rules. When gold fever came to the Rand, Rhodes and his associates were in on the ground floor and developed their gold mines following the same rules that had served them so well in Kimberly. But by then the threat of theft had nothing to do with their implementation.

After Cecil Rhodes died, Ernest Oppenheimer came to the fore and remade the South African diamond industry in his own image. Unlike Rhodes, whose agenda was political, Oppenheimer was purely a businessman interested in making money for its own sake. He began by forming a company to compete with De Beers and, with the support of such financiers as the Rothschilds and J.P. Morgan, eventually took over the De Beers giant as well as most of its other South African competitors. During the Great Depression of the 1930s, when the world's producers were flooding the market with diamonds, he took advantage of low prices to buy all he could, and at the depth of the Depression he formed the Diamond Producers Association with the aim of controlling the output of every diamond mine in the world and gaining the power to establish prices worldwide. Within a few years, De Beers and Oppenheimer's Anglo-American Trading Company controlled ninety-five percent of the world's diamond market, and Oppenheimer proudly stated that the remaining five percent was "negligible."

Some people say that the sun is trapped inside a diamond and that's what gives it its sparkle. Anyone who has ever visited South Africa's western Cape Province, where the world's best gem-quality diamonds come from, can easily believe it. There is brilliant sunshine to spare over plains where the land seems endless and the sky soars dramatically overhead. Its history is dramatic too, and reminders of it are as much a part of the landscape as those alluvial diamonds that once prompted men who couldn't spell the word "geologist" to study every rock in sight. There are ghost towns out there where diggers still have "an eye to the main chance," sometimes succeeding, and there are deep holes that serve as monuments to those who didn't.

A wide open plain extends across the Orange River into the Orange Free State where the "main chance" is more likely to be in gold than diamonds. More than fifty-six percent of the world's gold is supplied by South Africa and about half the new deposits found each year lie across the seven districts that arc from the eastern Transvaal southward into the Free State. Prospectors began recovering gold from the northern fields in the 1880s, and it was discovered in the Orange Free State at the turn of the century. But discovering gold and getting rich from it are not necessarily the same thing. The men who found the reef were not sure how deep the vein was and so they couldn't interest any local bankers in financing a mine. Eventually they formed a syndicate and two of them headed for London on a fund-raising expedition. But their ship was wrecked, they were drowned, the syndicate was dissolved and the Free State gold rush was postponed for more than thirty years. Some attempts were made to probe for pay dirt during those years, but it wasn't until 1939 that the dream paid off with proof that the dreamers had been sitting on one of the richest goldfields in the world. World War II put their dream on hold for another seven years, but in the years since then, the Free State's only serious rival in the production of gold has been South Africa's own Witwatersrand.

Since the 1960s, some of South Africa's gold has been minted into one-ounce coins called Krugerrands. Like the country's silver coin worth one rand, it is engraved with the image of a springbok, South Africa's national emblem. There are thousands of these cousins of the gazelle in South Africa, but it found its way onto the country's coat of arms through a small herd in London Zoo.

When the South African rugby team went to England in 1906 it arrived without a nickname, much to the consternation of the sportswriters there. But those who went along with the team for an afternoon at the zoo were able to report a little bit of history in the making when the team's captain gathered them in front of the springbok pen and announced that his players wanted to be known as De Springbokken. Four years later the springbok joined its larger relative, the gemsbok, as the official symbol of the entire country.

Without the inspiration of the springbok's resemblance to an enthusiastic rugby player, officials would probably still be debating which animal most typifies South Africa. Spared that problem, they became early supporters of conservation, protecting and preserving their amazing variety of wildlife. They have been working at it for more than a hundred years. In fact, South Africa was one of the first countries to protect its animals, but in the beginning conservation in South Africa wasn't hailed as an idea for which the time had come. Some of the strongest opponents, in fact, were veterinarians and others who were recognized experts in the care and preservation of animal species.

The villain of the piece, to their way of thinking, was a tiny creature that had protected great herds of rhino and other animals from being wiped out by hunters, creating in the process a secure oasis for them in central Natal. The government was determined to turn the oasis into a game reserve, but the experts argued effectively that the only way to create a true Eden was to kill all the game animals first. The aforementioned villain was the tsetse fly. It protected herds of wild animals because its presence kept hunters away from the rich savannah in the former land of the Zulus just as it had discouraged white settlers – its bite resulted in sleeping sickness and certain death. There was neither a cure for the disease nor any known way to eliminate the flies, but scientists decided that without wild animals for them to feed on they would eventually disappear. And that was where matters stood in 1897 when the South African Government set aside the Umfolozi and Hluhluwe Game Reserves. Opposition in the scientific community was quieted by declaring them special experimental stations for the study of tsetse flies. Nonetheless, thousands of animals were slaughtered in the scientists' quest to eliminate the tsetse problem over the next few decades, but enough of the herds survived to make the Natal reserves serve their original purpose after the discovery of DDT in the mid-1940s put an end to the tsetse menace forever.

The South African game reserves are surely the most fascinating and probably the best managed in Africa or anywhere else in the world. Possibly the best testimonial of South African success was given by the case of a lion who was born in Mozambique in the early 1950s. He wandered down into Natal, where no lion had been spotted in a half-century, and eventually found his way into the Umfolozi Reserve. The animals there had never encountered a lion before so he had no problem keeping well fed and showed no inclination to go back home again. Within a few years several female lions managed to make their way across the open farm country. If the trailblazer had been entertaining any thoughts of leaving, they were forgotten then. There are now more than fifty lions sharing the reserve with black and white rhino, giraffes, leopards, hippopotamuses, zebras, antelope and more than three hundred different kinds of birds.

There are more than four hundred and fifty species of birds in Kruger National Park, which was created from a wildlife sanctuary established in eastern Transvaal by President Paul Kruger in 1898, just twenty-six years after the world's first national park was established at Yellowstone in the United States. It has become the standard for all the game parks in Africa and, although some may be bigger and others wilder, Kruger supports the greatest variety of wildlife species on the entire continent. Almost no visitor goes away without having seen a herd of elephants and few will have missed seeing at least one pride of lions. Giraffes are easier to spot, of course, as are the zebras and the bounding impalas. A leopard or a cheetah may be camera shy, but there are enough of them for the sharp-eyed to take home memories of seeing them in the wild.

Occasionally wild animals have been known to come

out of the wilderness for a taste of civilization. It happened back in 1928 when an adventuresome hippopotamus began a three-year journey down the coast from Zululand. Almost the entire population of South Africa became involved after the animal crashed its way through a sugar cane plantation in Natal and newspapers picked up the trail. They decided to name the hippo Hubert, but when it was discovered that "he" was really a "she," the name was changed to Huberta. But a hippo by any name is a creature to be reckoned with and Huberta began by disrupting train and bus schedules – not because she got in the way, but because passengers demanded a closer look. Her wanderings became a subject of national pride. The Indian population of the Holiday Coast gave her the status of a goddess, as did the Zulu, who were convinced that she was a reincarnation of their legendary Chief Shaka. The Government officially declared her royal game after she demonstrated mild irritation at being trailed by a hunting party determined to capture her as a mate for a hippo in the Johannesburg Zoo – a fool's errand as it turned out, because the zoo-bound hippo was a female too.

Huberta was showered with food wherever she went and when she reached the Wild Coast, the Pondo people there looked the other way when she wallowed among their crops because they too believed she was a divine creature. Huberta was so well treated at Durban that she decided to spend the winter there. As a parting shot, she crashed the 1929 April Fool's Day dance at the Durban Golf Club. It must have been a terrific party because she spent the night apparently sleeping it off in the doorway of a local drugstore.

Her journey took her as far as East London where she finally met an untimely end in the nearby Keiskamma River, the victim of a hunting party's guns. The sportsmen killers were tracked down, but the only punishment the law prescribed was a stiff fine. The hunters pleaded that they had never heard of Huberta or her adventures, a story which to this day no one in South Africa really believes.

From Zoar a branch road northeast to Prince Albert traverses the Seweweekspoort Pass (facing page), also known as Seven Weeks Poort, past the Seweweekspoort Mountain which, at over 2,000 feet tall, is the highest peak in the Klein Swartberg range. The pass is said to be haunted by the ghost of an old toll keeper swinging his lantern in search of brandy smugglers. Amid the rush of wind, echoes and chatter of running water, it is easy to believe in him. The original toll house is still in place.

Facing page: the sands of the Kalahari Desert in the Northern Cape (these pages and overleaf). The remarkable San people inhabit the desert, subsisting mainly on plant matter, such as the tsamma melon. They are a lean, extraordinarily fit people, and deadly accurate shots. However, they only ever take enough from the land for their survival, believing that to misuse their environment will incur the wrath of the Supreme Being. Laurens van der Post, in his book The Lost World of the Kalahari, describes San tracking game on the run as far as thirty kilometres and then sprinting to the kill. Above: lions of the Kalahari. The male has a characteristic tawny-coloured mane, which differentiates him from lions outside the area. Above right: springbok, the animal emblem of South Africa, in the Kalahari's Gemsbok National Park. This park is named after the long-horned antelope (right) that can survive months of desert aridity without water. Blue wildebeest (below) also flourish here. Below right: arid land near Upington. Overleaf: Augrabies Falls, at which point the Orange River plunges 650 feet. The Khoikhoi called this place Aukoerebis, 'the place of the great noise'. At peak flood about 405 million litres of water rush over the falls every minute, producing nineteen separate waterfalls.

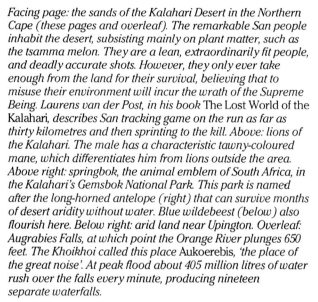

Facing page: the bronze statue at Kimberley Mine, commemorating the diamond miners who worked there. Kimberley, 'the diamond city', grew up around 'Big Hole' (above) – the original, now disused, Old Kimberley Mine. Diamonds were discovered there in the late 1800s and, in 1871, the New Rush sent a wave of prospectors to Colesberg Koppie, as the area of the Big Hole was then called. Thirty thousand men burrowed into the earth in a mass of mining activity. Cecil Rhodes brought some order to the proceedings by founding the De Beers Consolidated Mines Ltd. (overleaf), an organisation that came to dominate the world trade in diamonds. Above right and below right: Kimberley's open-air museum. Right: an information signpost. Below: the Wesselton Mine, bought by Rhodes from Pieter Wessels in 1891 for £451,438. Wessels used his money to fund the Seven Day Adventists.

SECTION LOOKING EAST

The Kimberley Mine
DISCOVERED 16TH JULY 1871 BY FLEETWOOD RAWSTORNE

AREA AT SURFACE	17 ha
PERIMETER	1,6 km
AXIS NORTH & SOUTH	500 m
AXIS EAST & WEST	457 m
SURFACE TO TOP OF HARD ROCK	90 m
SURFACE TO WATER	165 m
DEPTH OF WATER	230 m
GROUND EXCAVATED	22,500,000 t
DIAMONDS PRODUCED	14,504,566 carats
EQUIVALENT TO	2722 kg
WORKING CEASED	AUGUST 1914

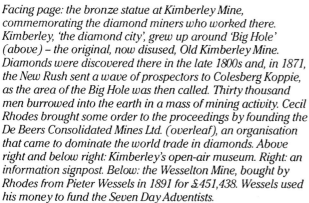

Above: sculpture in the Civic Centre of Cape Town (these pages). Below: the Houses of Parliament, built in 1884. Facing page: City Hall, built to a prize-winning design submitted in 1893 by Reid and Green, Johannesburg architects. Work was finished in 1905. It overlooks the daily fruit and flower market of Grand Parade. Overleaf: Clifton, Camps Bay and the Twelve Apostles Mountains of the Cape. These sandstone buttresses, stretching from Camps Bay to Llandudno, were named by British Governor Sir Rufane Donkin.

Paarl, the place where the Afrikaans language evolved and headquarters of the Wine Farmer's Co-operative (KWV), stands on the banks of the Berg (facing page). Above: the memorial to the Franschhoek Huguenots who contributed much to local viniculture. Above right: Worcester, on the Breë River, at the head of Hex River Valley, named for a witch – 'hex' – said to haunt the mountains in search of a lost lover. The story is told of a great beauty, Eliza Meiring, who was besieged by suitors. Exasperated, she declared that she would marry none but the man who could bring her a disa of a type that grew only on the most treacherous mountain heights. When a suitor died in the attempt, Eliza, guilt-ridden, suffered a breakdown and eventually killed herself. Right: a Cape-Dutch-gable-style house in Tulbagh. Below right: the nineteenth-century Theological Seminary at Stellenbosch (overleaf), and (below) the Burger House on the River Braak.

*Above: ostriches, and (above left) sheep on the Little Karoo.
Left: ostrich chicks at Highgate ostrich farm in Oudshoorn. The
Little Karoo was as profitable to couturiers as Kimberley was to
jewellers. Ostrich feathers were exported to fashion houses the
world over by people who became known as 'feather barons'.
Nearby lies the Cango Crocodile Ranch (below left). Below:
farmland near the Karoo. Facing page: (bottom) the landscape
near Oudsthoorn, and (top) the Cango Caves at Oudsthoorn.
The first white man to stumble upon them was a herdsman
following a wounded buck in 1780. The San knew of the caves
long before, but without reliable sources of light had not
explored very far. Torches and water pumps revealed cavern
upon cavern. In 1938 the caves were proclaimed a national
monument to protect formations over 150,000 years old.*

Facing page top: the steam trains of Wilderness (facing page bottom, above right, right and below). Coming into Wilderness, the trains take a very scenic crossing over the mouth of the Kaaimans River (below right) – kaaimans being Hottentot for crocodile. Above: Tsitsikama Forest National Park between Knysna and Port Elizabeth. Overleaf: the Heads, Knysna Cape, two great sandstone cliffs at the entrance of Knysna Lagoon. Knysna was founded in 1804 by George Rex, said to have been the son of George III of England from a morganatic marriage to the beautiful Quaker, Hannah Lightfoot. By this style of marriage Hannah and George had no rights to George III's position or inheritance. Consequently George Rex arrived at the Cape in 1797 in banishment when his royal father unexpectedly acceded to the throne.

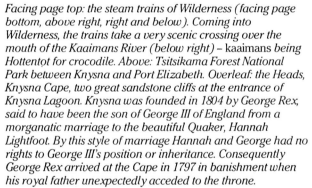

Facing page: (top) City Hall, and (bottom) the Donkin Reserve, both in Port Elizabeth. The town was named after founder Sir Rufane Donkin's wife. Addo (above), near Port Elizabeth, is the site of the Addo Elephant National Park, which protects the rare small, reddish Addo elephant. Right: scenic Baviaanskloof, baboon gorge, west of Port Elizabeth. Below: the Valley of Desolation, where tall, craggy pinnacles overlook Graaff-Reinet and the Karoo. Overleaf: the town hall of Graaff-Reinet, constructed in 1910 on Church Square. The town was founded in 1786 by Dutch East India Governor Cornelius Jacob van de Graaff, whose wife's maiden name was Reinet. The town's buildings include more than 200 national monuments.

Above: Zulu rickshaw pullers dressed in traditional beadwork and modern footwear, illustrating one of the anomalies of modern South Africa. Above left and overleaf: City Hall, and (left) the modern hotels of Durban (these pages). Below left: 'Golden Mile' beachfront. Below: the 1897 Vasco Da Gama Clock, a present to Durban from the Portuguese Government. Vasco Da Gama sighted and named Natal on Christmas Day, 1497. Facing page: (top) the yacht harbour, and (bottom) North Beach washed by the Indian Ocean.

Facing page: (top) Royal Natal National Park Hotel against the curved mountain known as the Amphitheatre, and (bottom) Champagne Castle in the Drakensberg Mountains, on the borders of Natal and Lesotho, in Royal Natal National Park (these pages and overleaf). Above: the Cascades, and (above right) the Sentinel. Right: Drakensberg Garden, and (below and below right) Tugela Gorge. Overleaf: Mlambonya River, traversing the Cathedral Peak area. The park became 'Royal' in 1947 when the British Royal Family paid a visit to the area.

Below: First National House and the Stock Exchange in Johannesburg (these pages and overleaf). Facing page: downtown, dominated by Hillbrow's J.G. Strijdom Post Office Tower. Overleaf: the city seen from Langermans Kop, Kensington. Penniless Australian prospector George Harrison found gold here in 1886, then he just disappeared, later selling his claim to one of the world's richest veins for £10. In his absence a gold town boomed, eventually named for two civil servants called Johannes.

Sir Herbert Baker's grand Union Buildings (left and below left), built on Meintjieskop, overlook the city of Pretoria (these pages), the bronze of General Louis Botha (overleaf) prominent among the statuary. Another equestrian statue in the grounds is a replica of the Delville Wood Memorial (bottom left and below), commemorating the 2,683 South African soldiers who died at Delville Wood in the First World War.

Facing page: (top) Pretoria (these pages), seen beyond jacaranda trees, and (bottom) Church Square, with Anton van Wouw's bronze of President Kruger in the centre. Below: the Voortrekker Monument to the Afrikaner pioneers who settled this part of South Africa during the nineteenth century. One of them, Andries Pretorius, established a farm on the site of today's capital. On November 16th, 1855, his son, Marthinus, named the town that had sprung up there in honour of his father.

Below: the Three Rondavels, Blyde River Canyon (these pages), eastern Transvaal. In the winter of 1840, Voortrekker Hendrik Potgietr led a party of pioneers to the Portuguese port of Lourenco Marques, leaving their women behind in the malaria-free Drakensbergs. These women waited and waited for Hendrik's return, then, finally deciding he and his fellows had died, set off home. They were overtaken by the returning pioneers at the ford of a river which they named Blyde, 'joy', in celebration.

Below: Elands River and Valley, Eastern Transvaal (these pages), and (right) the landscape around God's Window. Below right: autumn near Pilgrim's Rest, and (bottom right) bougainvillea near Abel Erasmus Pass, named for a nineteenth-century pioneer of the lowveld. The first occupant of Pilgrim's Rest was Wheelbarrow Alec Patterson, so called because he carried all his belongings in a barrow. He panned the stream there, finding a rich gold deposit. William Trafford, who joined him later, named it.

Facing page: (top) a leopard in the Transvaal's Kruger National Park, and (bottom) a lion in Londolozi Game Reserve. Above: an African elephant, protected in the game parks of South Africa, but still endangered. Above right: a kudu bull feeding in the Milwane Game Reserve, and (right) Burchell's zebra. Bottom right: rhino, and (below) a giraffe, both in the privately owned Sabi Sabi game ranch in the Transvaal lowveld. Overleaf: a cheetah in Kruger National Park.